La Luna Llena

La Luna Llena

Presentation by *BookLeaf Publishing*

Web: www.bookleafpub.com

E-mail: info@bookleafpub.com

ISBN: 9789357616560

First edition 2022

Hiva and Kuhane

You and me are like the stars in the sky

Watching the world go by

You are the sun, the moon in my sky

You are the light in my life, my child

You are the light in my life

Harvest Moon

You grew a piece of my heart from seed
With your love pure as rain
Your kindness was the warmth of the sun
So this piece, it sings your name

In your memory it peacefully grows
Nourished from the purity it holds
Enough to last a thousand years
This seed, this piece of my soul

When the memories faded I thought it had died
But there it still grows to my deepest surprise
In the quietest corner where it patiently lies
It held my gaze, my tear-wet eyes

Maybe you forgot this seed
Assumed that it had gone to weed?
Perhaps you'd find it hard to believe
Because it was me that left your heart to bleed

But you were not the only hand
To hold this piece of love so grand
The years have passed love, but understand
Your seed grew roots and claimed this land

So now, sweet friend, let me explain
The effect of your love that was pure as rain
The way it can still wash away pain
And remind me of my roots again

Like words that remind us we're not alone
Like a warm sun ray on a winter's day
What a beautiful gift my soul has known
This piece of my heart that love has grown!

Blue Moon

I see you there
As the sun goes down
Your wings are open wide and free
And you fly heaven bound

Your mind is clear
Like the sky is after rain
You know that where you're going
Means you've left behind the pain

So take with you our love
Feel it flowing like the flood
Of tears we cry for you

And no longer feel the cold
As you reunite with your soul
And know that we remember only beauty

Just like a butterfly
Painted colours bright and bold
Your creation was a gift of grace
Never meaning to grow old

But now you've flown away
To be born again some day

Only you know your way
To freedom, peace and happiness

Blood Moon

So tired in my brain
Going to burst from the strain
Feeling good intentions drain
Will I ever feel sane, again?

I want to close my eyes
Escape this love and all its lies
No more time for selfish cries
Manifesting sad goodbyes

In ugly mud I'm sinking fast
Loosing faith that good things last
Splintered sharp like broken glass
I want to slink back to my past

I was a bird, but now a cage
I've trapped myself on this weathered page
Feeling frustrations turn to rage
Just too young to feel so aged

In the mirror I avoid looking deep
Seeing things once valued, now cheap
Sad to see eyes too ready to weep
A solemn face masking terror beneath.

Butterfly Moon

Have you ever held a butterfly
In your hand, it tickles your skin
How you'd like to hold such beauty close
To fondly admire her wings

Have you ever held a butterfly
"Come look at this!" you command
You yearn to share your treasure
This world of beauty in your hand

Have you ever held a butterfly
Wanted to keep it, watch it grow
Afraid to open up your hand in case
She flies where you can't go

Have you ever held a butterfly
You know wasn't yours to own
So you say goodbye, your love the breeze
That helps her fly back home

Lunar Eclipse

Oh Sister, oh sister, where do we begin
For your role in my person bleeds over the brim
You tested the womb, you claimed it as yours
And programmed its owner to look for my flaws

Oh sister, Oh sister, you did try your best
On rotting foundations you furnished your nest
Was I just too clean of our parent's past?
An image too crisp and not dirty enough?

Was I too pretty, too tall or too weak?
Too authentic, uncluttered when I tried to speak?
Through your bitterness I grew like a sickly seed
I could not see my flower, when you saw a weed

Oh sister, we've grown, and so has our love
Though deep in my heart lies these feelings
untouched
I'd stored them on rafters unreachably high
I thought "out of sight", yet they play with my
mind

Oh sister, Oh sister, our future is bright
But first you must own this theft of my light
I ask your reflection to un-eclipse my moon
So we may shine equally outside of the womb

Flower Moon

I stand in a field of Californian Poppies
They sway in the ripple of the breeze
I sway in the breeze
I am also the poppies

They feel my humanity
They are also part me
As the sun imparts its warmth
To our delicate petals

For I am the poppies
I am also the sun, loving me
I am also the breeze that kisses my face
For she loves me, and I love myself

We relish in our combined silence
Our joined consciousness
So this is what it feels like, to be alive.
To be alive

Wolf Moon

We should have wailed with you, woman.
Screamed, keened, helped you weep.
We should have wailed with you woman,
A vocal vortex for your grief.

We should have wailed with you, woman.
Given your grief a warm home.
We should have waded into your river, woman.
So you didn't float alone.

We should have wailed with you, woman.
Howled together at the moon.
We should have freed your wild beast, woman.
So your aching grief could bloom.

We should have wailed with you, woman.
As one cacophony of love and fear.
We should have wailed with you, woman.
For all the young girls to hear.

Super Moon

Excuse me, dear Sir
Did you misjudge my depth?
As you stumble to retrace
Your shallow steps

I assure you your radar
Has not been mistaken
You've just entered the womb
Of the female forsaken

New Moon

He responds to her suffering like a moth to a
flame
And she soaks up his spirit like a drought
touching rain
For suppressed in her soul lies generations of
pain
Of men, who hid females in houses of shame.

But not this one, I observe, who seems unlike his
brother
He approaches with reverence, like a son to his
mother
He touches her shoulder like a compassionate
lover
Then he exits the womb, to attend to another.

In the simplest of actions his wake felt profound
Like a new earth emerging through trembling
ground
A new song, two harmonies of equal sound
Of sons born again, to their fathers unbound.

Honey Moon

12

Her smile fans across the milky way space
Stardust settling like dancing glitter
Her eyes akin to a world of their own
How blessed I am to share this world with her

She punches out of the cradling nest
Determined to change the perception of fate
Slender limbed with robust heart
She'll change the vibration for universe sake

Sun Moon

13

Into the night his hungry soul flies
An appetite for truth alive in his eyes
His birth place ablaze, there's no going home
A refuge crossing borders, alone

The green of his eyes the most verdant truth
Striking me down with rebellious youth
With my love as fuel he'll douse us with flames
Like the phoenix arisen from ashes of shame

Womb Moon

I place my heart under the tap
To fill her with The River
The River of Knowing and Trust
For her clarity is a life-giver

My fears lay unfounded
Though they whisper the stakes
Watch how I shush them
In the silence of my wake

My intentions have roots
Tied to the core of the earth
Stability, empowerment, warmth
Boundary my hearth

I ask that you now
As our hearts do align
Join this River of Knowing
This Knowing of mine

Dark Moon

Excuse me excusing, please
Excavated memories of a disease
Pulling me down to my knees
Sorry for your time, excuse me please

Why did my lioness concede?
Bow my head, reframe the sick
This pain has its own mind
Stored in my heart, leg and wrists

This store of abuse
Somewhere in my flesh
The excuses they rot
In my heart enmeshed

Why did I store these away?
These feelings of guilt, present today
He was awful to me, but I stayed
The shame compounds in every way

These feelings like hairballs
Choke as they lodge in my neck
Please no more today I ask
I'm tired, let me rest

Waxing Moon

Water
Just like water
Love like water
For a thirty heart

Water
You're like water
Clear clean water
Clear clean love

Floating
On your water
Safe and weightless
In your arms

Season's change
But your water
Keeps flowing
A gentle flood

I'll travel surely
In your river
Because in your water
I believe in love

Crescent Moon

17

All souls are born beautiful
In a package of soft skin
It's the way that they're nurtured
That kindles the brilliance within

For a woman such as you
A fiercely loving mother and friend
This soul in your arms
Is a gift to the world, lovingly opened

Cocoon Moon

"Let me know if you need anything"
He'd say with a smile and a nod
Well I need you to live forever, Poppy
I can't face a world with you gone

"Do you need any money?"
He would say on repeat
For his girls can't go wanting
While he still had a heartbeat

"The test of a man is not in easy times"
He'd say with compassionate eyes
Supporting my choices, even when wrong
The sweetest, most fiercest ally

When we were with you Poppy
We were the sun, you the moon
No ulterior motive surpassed
Your role as a loving cocoon

How I wish I could bottle
All you were as a man
Pour you into the world, Poppy
To bask in your magic again

If talking is silver and listening is gold
You were richer than anyone knew
If I know what to treasure in this life, Poppy
That's because I was blessed to have you

Eternal Moon

There is no time's end
That will extinguish this flame
It was forged in the stars
Before the earth knew our names

We expand and retract
In our movements together
The world ambles on
But our stardust is tethered

In your shooting star life
You left quite the wake
The bittersweet eye blink
For universe sake

So when earth-life feels dark
I place my wick to your flame
For I know you'll ignite me
Our stardust the same

La Luna Llena

La Luna Llena, the full moon
My heart is bursting with you
You glisten the pine trees
And I feel your glowing praise

Though, this poem is not about you
In spite of our love
It's for the majesty that you backlight
The pines, the pines

You see the connection
My trunk is her trunk
My hair is her lichen
Her green scales my skin

The smell of her needles
Piercing my doubts
For we were destined to be
Sisters in arms

The green of her scales
Is the colour of my day sky
Nightly she is my silhouette
Thrown from your starry throne

Lying under her brethren
From when I was a child
There is nothing of her
That I don't love

You have both held us
My heart and my people
For generations gone
And many more to come

La Luna Lena
In your full light we bask
The Pines, The Pines
In your branches we trust